# 1 Vertical Lines

■ Draw a line from one picture to the matching picture.

Name

Date

W9-BIN-545

**To parents**
Write your child's name and the date in the boxes above. Line drawing exercises help your child to develop basic pencil-control skills. Encourage your child to draw lines carefully.

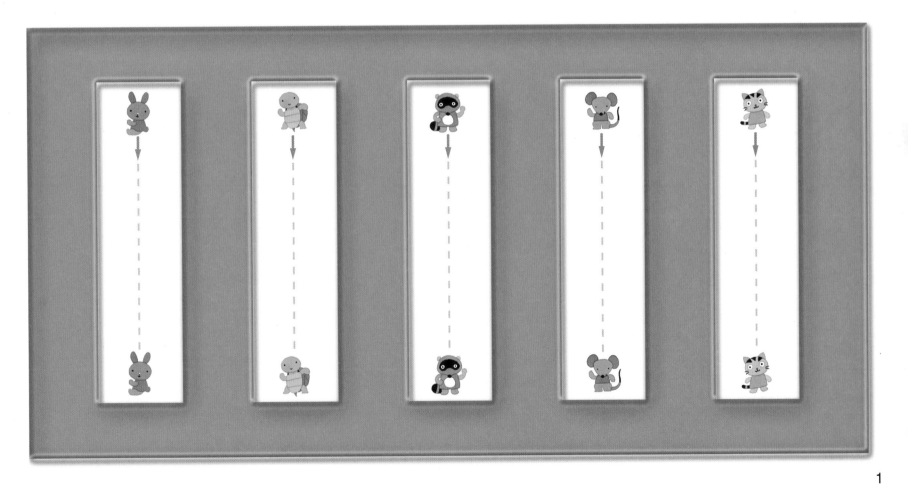

■ Draw a line from one picture to the matching picture.

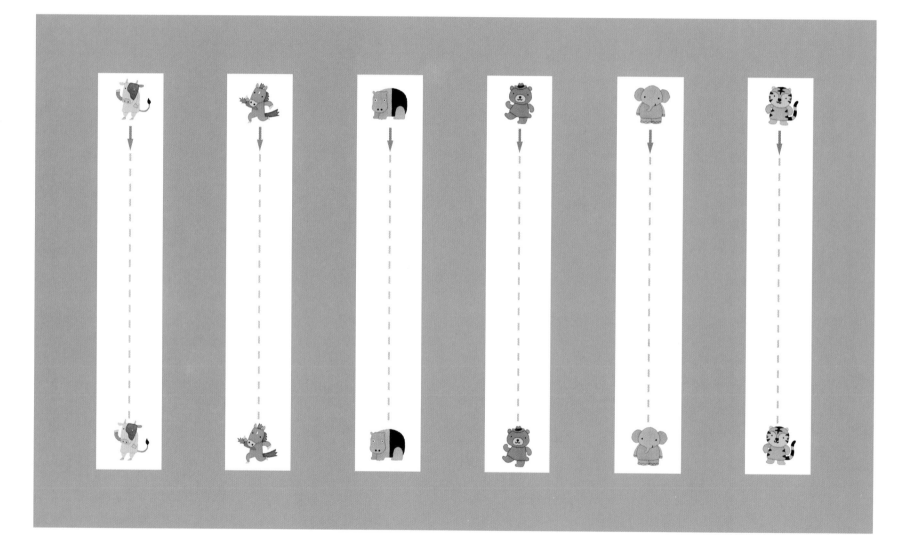

# 2 Horizontal Lines

Name

Date

■ Draw a line from one picture to the matching picture.

■ Draw a line from one picture to the matching picture.

4

## 3 Writing L

- Read the word aloud and trace the letters.

Name

Date

**To parents**
Before your child begins writing, please read the vocabulary word and ask your child to repeat the word after you. If your child can recognize the letter, it might be fun to ask him or her to tell you the name and sound of each letter while he or she traces it.

L    LION

A B C D E F G H I J K L M N O P Q R S T U V W X Y Z

# Writing T

■ Read the word aloud and trace the letters. Follow the order of the numbers.

T   Tomato

| A | B | C | D | E | F | G | H | I | J | K | L | M | N | O | P | Q | R | S | T | U | V | W | X | Y | Z |

| Name |
|---|
| Date |

■ Read the word aloud and trace the letters. Follow the order of the numbers.

H Hat

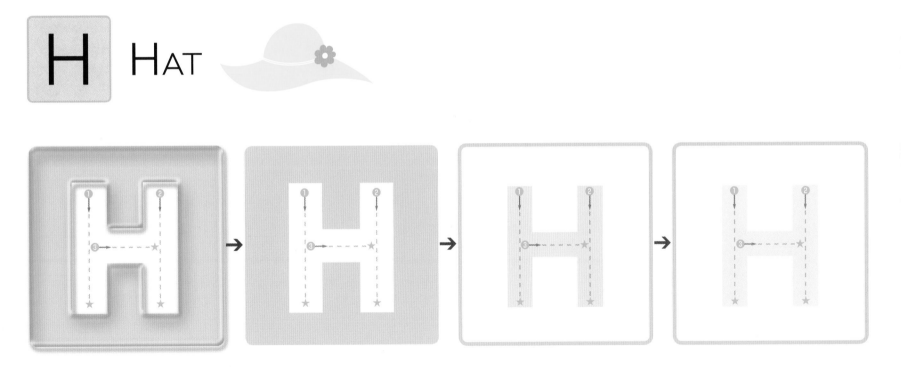

A B C D E F G H I J K L M N O P Q R S T U V W X Y Z

# Writing L, T, and H

■ Read the words aloud and trace the letters. Follow the order of the numbers.

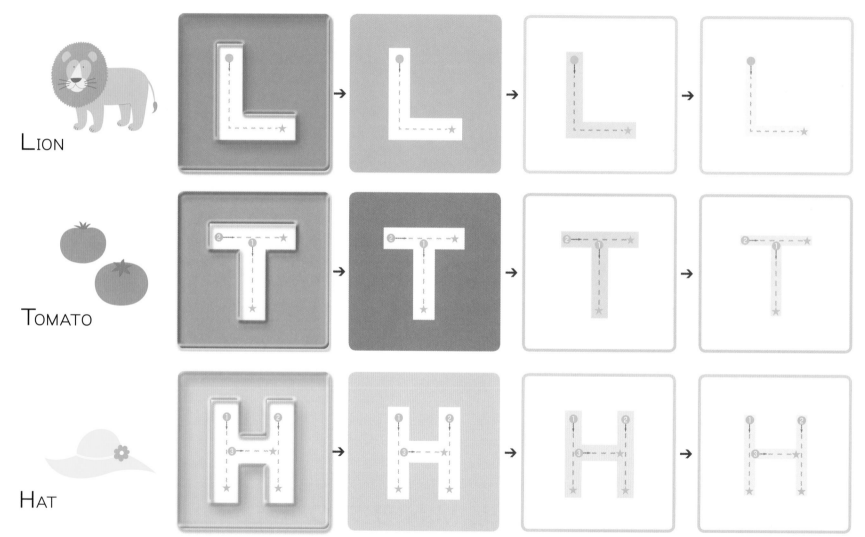

LION

TOMATO

HAT

## 5 Writing I

■ Read the word aloud and trace the letters. Follow the order of the numbers.

I ICE

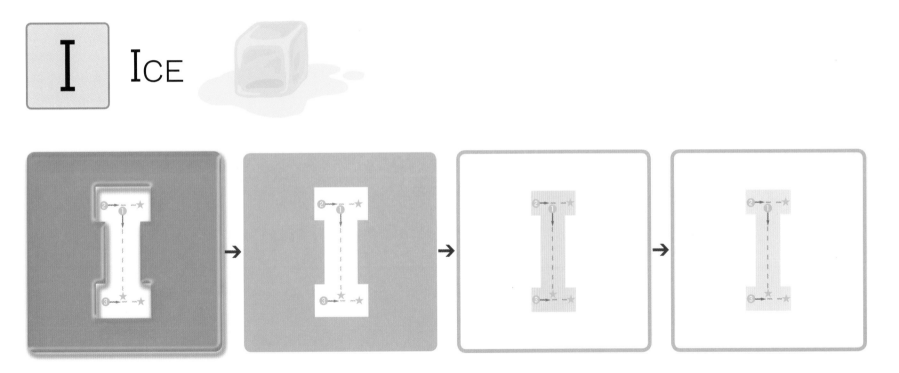

| A | B | C | D | E | F | G | H | I | J | K | L | M | N | O | P | Q | R | S | T | U | V | W | X | Y | Z |

9

# Writing F

■ Read the word aloud and trace the letters. Follow the order of the numbers.

F Fox

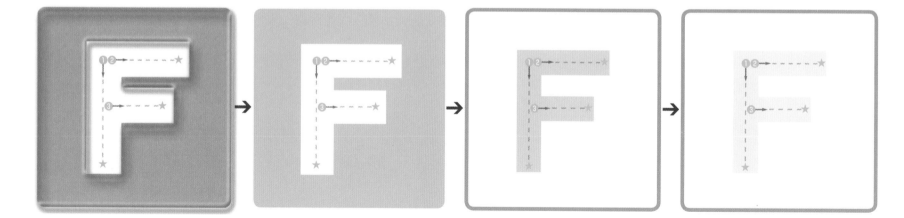

| A | B | C | D | E | F | G | H | I | J | K | L | M | N | O | P | Q | R | S | T | U | V | W | X | Y | Z |

| Name |
| --- |
| Date |

■ Read the word aloud and trace the letters. Follow the order of the numbers.

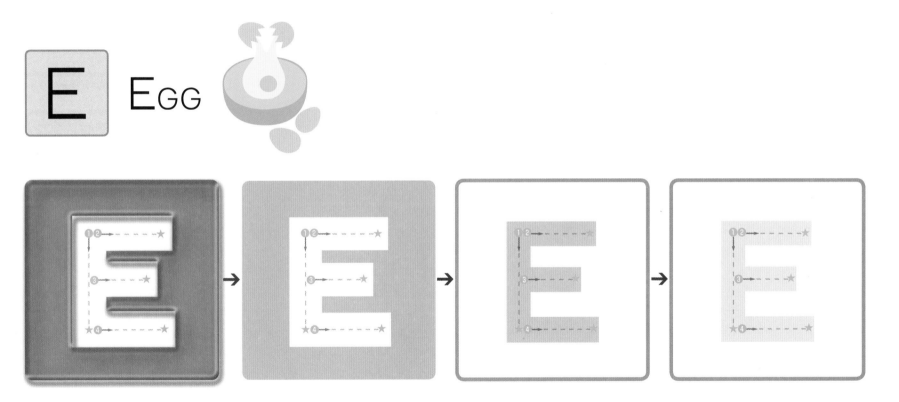

E   Egg

| A | B | C | D | E | F | G | H | I | J | K | L | M | N | O | P | Q | R | S | T | U | V | W | X | Y | Z |

# Writing I, F, and E

■ Read the words aloud and trace the letters. Follow the order of the numbers.

ICE

FOX

EGG

# 7 Diagonal Lines

■ Draw a line from one picture to the matching picture.

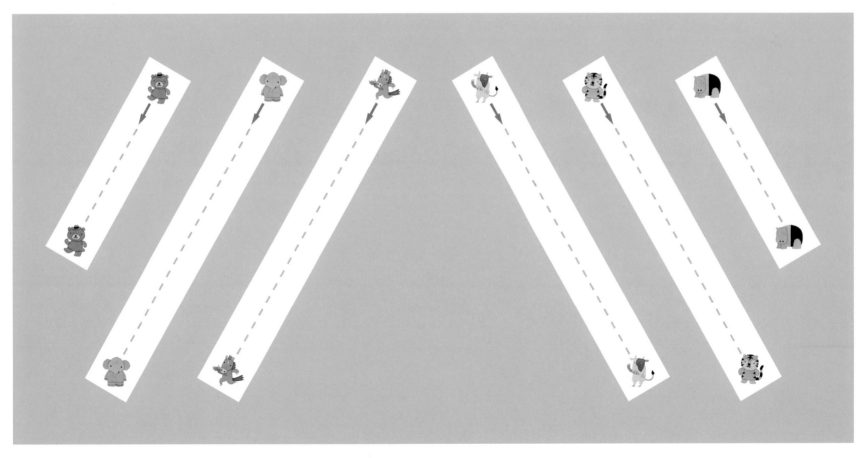

■ Draw a line from one picture to the matching picture.

# 8 Zigzag Lines

■ Draw a line from one picture to the matching picture.

■ Draw a line from one picture to the matching picture.

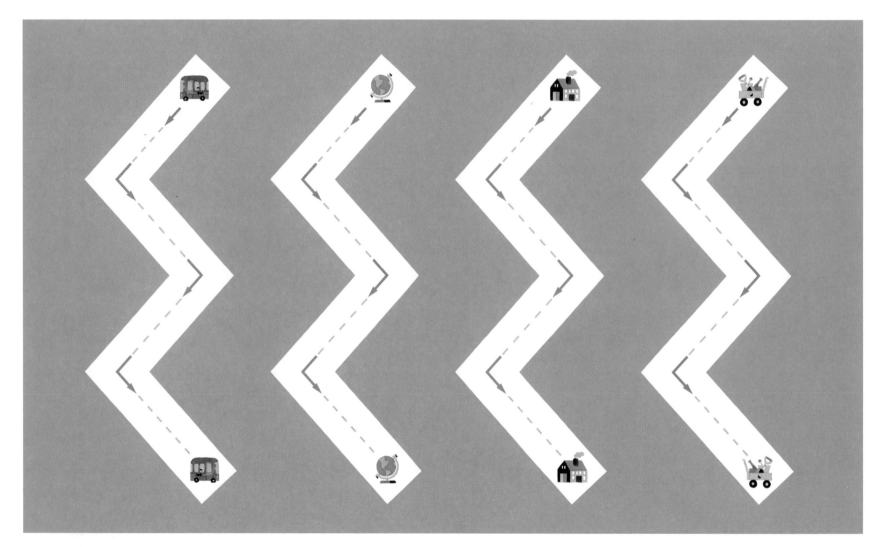

## Writing X

Name

Date

■ Read the word aloud and trace the letters. Follow the order of the numbers.

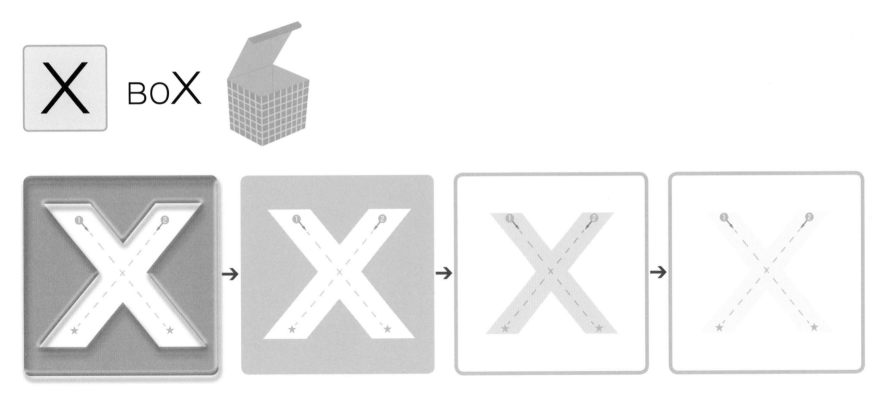

X    BOX

A B C D E F G H I J K L M N O P Q R S T U V W X Y Z

# Writing V

■ Read the word aloud and trace the letters.

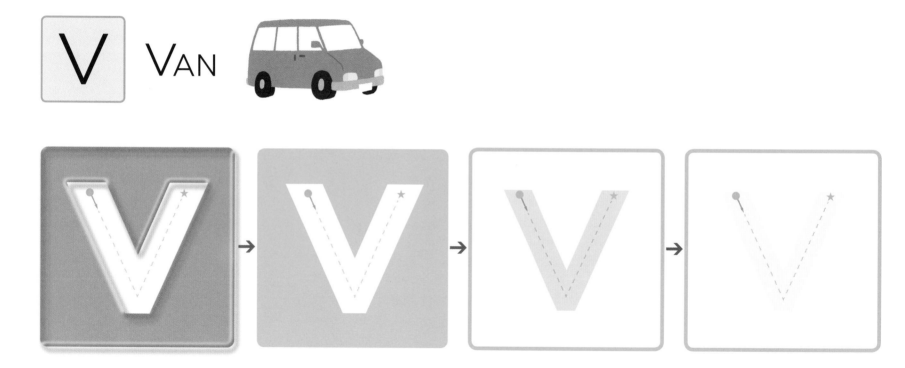

V  VAN

| A | B | C | D | E | F | G | H | I | J | K | L | M | N | O | P | Q | R | S | T | U | V | W | X | Y | Z |

**10** **Writing Y**

| Name |
|------|
| Date |

■ Read the word aloud and trace the letters. Follow the order of the numbers.

Y YAM

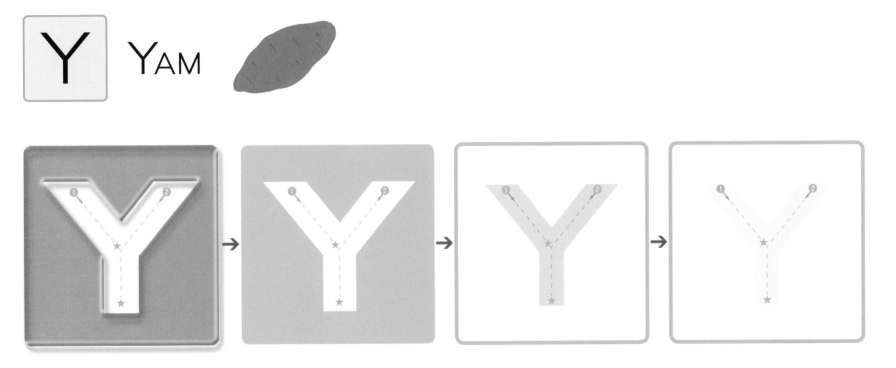

| A | B | C | D | E | F | G | H | I | J | K | L | M | N | O | P | Q | R | S | T | U | V | W | X | Y | Z |

# Writing X, V, and Y

■ Read the words aloud and trace the letters. Follow the order of the numbers.

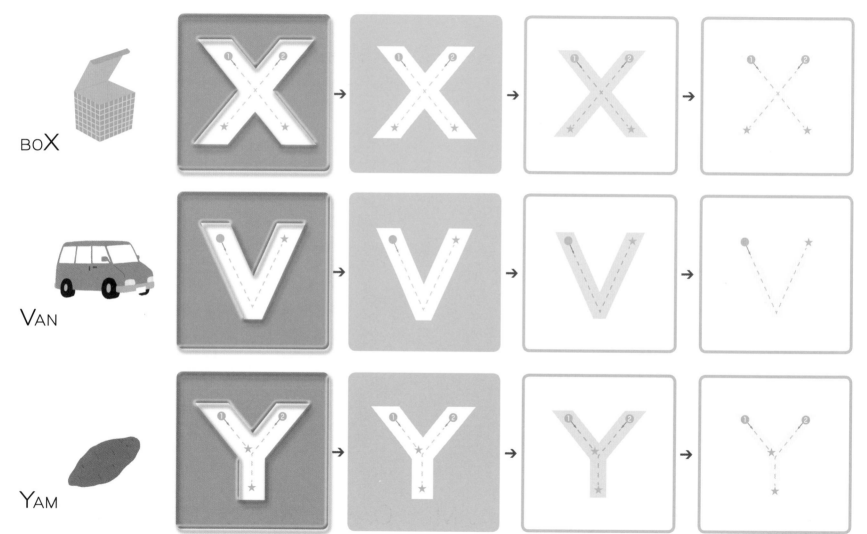

BOX

VAN

YAM

# Writing N

■ Read the word aloud and trace the letters. Follow the order of the numbers.

N  Nose

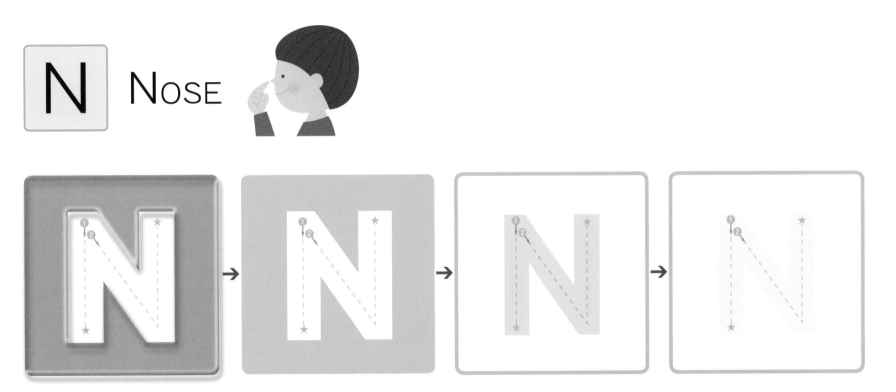

| A | B | C | D | E | F | G | H | I | J | K | L | M | N | O | P | Q | R | S | T | U | V | W | X | Y | Z |

# Writing Z

■ Read the word aloud and trace the letters.

Z  ZEBRA

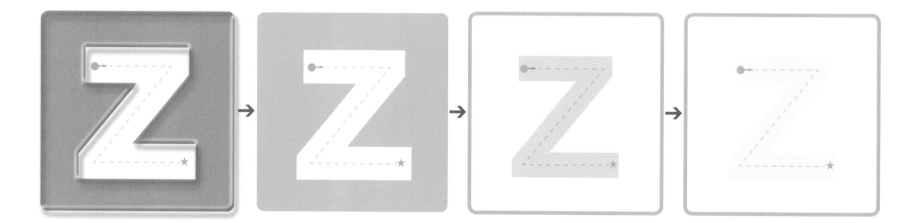

| A | B | C | D | E | F | G | H | I | J | K | L | M | N | O | P | Q | R | S | T | U | V | W | X | Y | Z |

# Writing A

■ Read the word aloud and trace the letters. Follow the order of the numbers.

A  APPLE

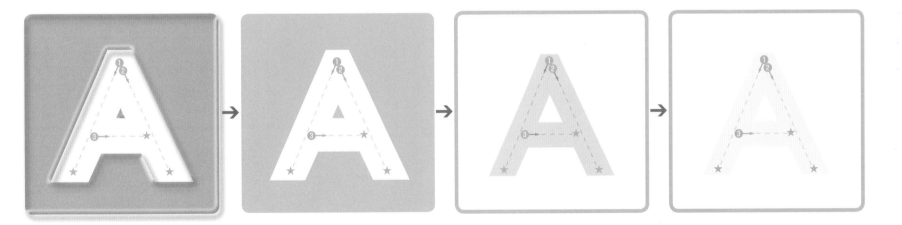

A B C D E F G H I J K L M N O P Q R S T U V W X Y Z

# Writing N, Z, and A

■ Read the words aloud and trace the letters. Follow the order of the numbers.

Nose

Zebra

Apple

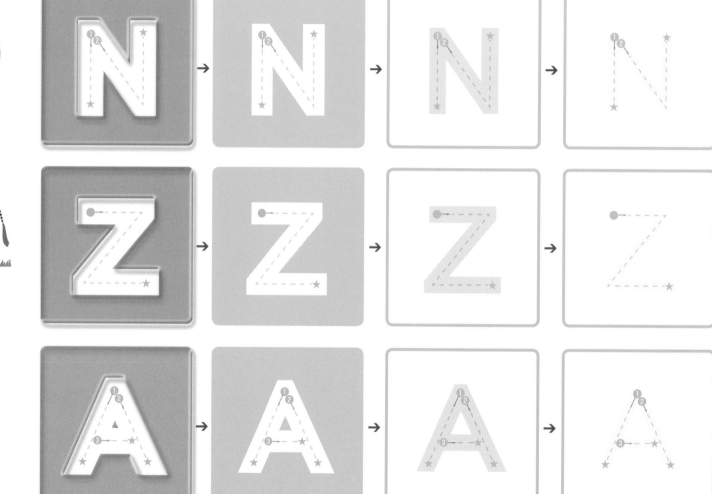

## 13 Writing K

Name

Date

■ Read the word aloud and trace the letters. Follow the order of the numbers.

K KEY

| A | B | C | D | E | F | G | H | I | J | K | L | M | N | O | P | Q | R | S | T | U | V | W | X | Y | Z |

# Writing M

■ Read the word aloud and trace the letters. Follow the order of the numbers.

M MILK

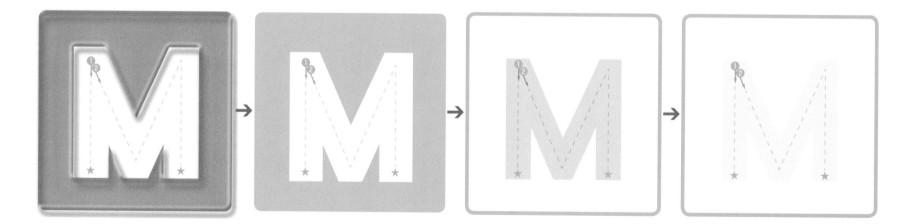

A B C D E F G H I J K L M N O P Q R S T U V W X Y Z

## Writing W

Name

Date

■ Read the word aloud and trace the letters.

W  WATER

| A | B | C | D | E | F | G | H | I | J | K | L | M | N | O | P | Q | R | S | T | U | V | W | X | Y | Z |

# Writing K, M, and W

■ Read the words aloud and trace the letters. Follow the order of the numbers.

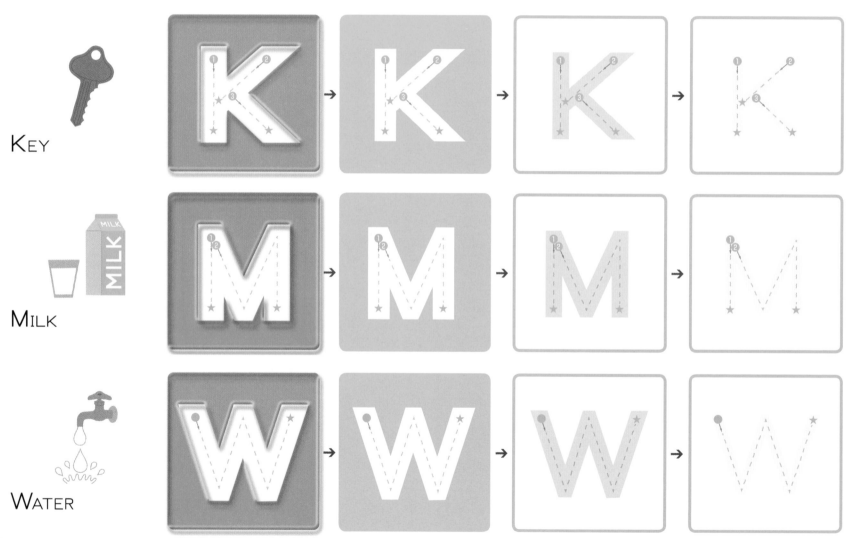

KEY

MILK

WATER

28

# Review: Writing L, T, H, and I

Name

Date

■ Read the words aloud and trace the letters. Follow the order of the numbers.

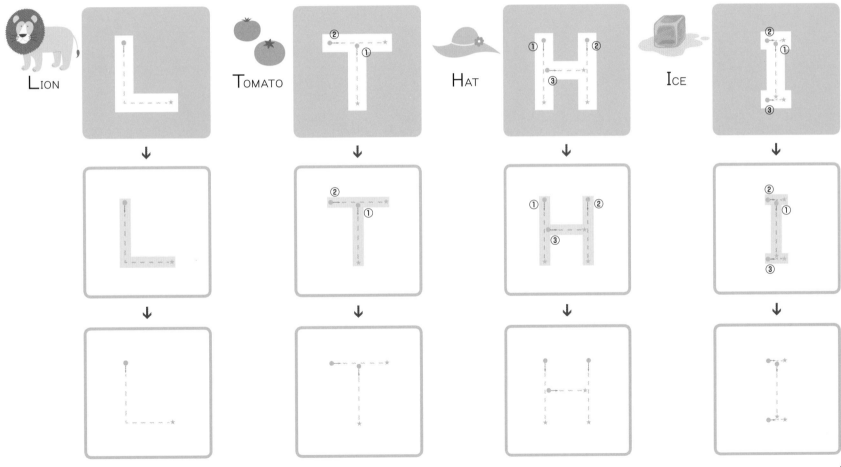

Lion    Tomato    Hat    Ice

# Review: Writing F, E, X, and V

■ Read the words aloud and trace the letters. Follow the order of the numbers.

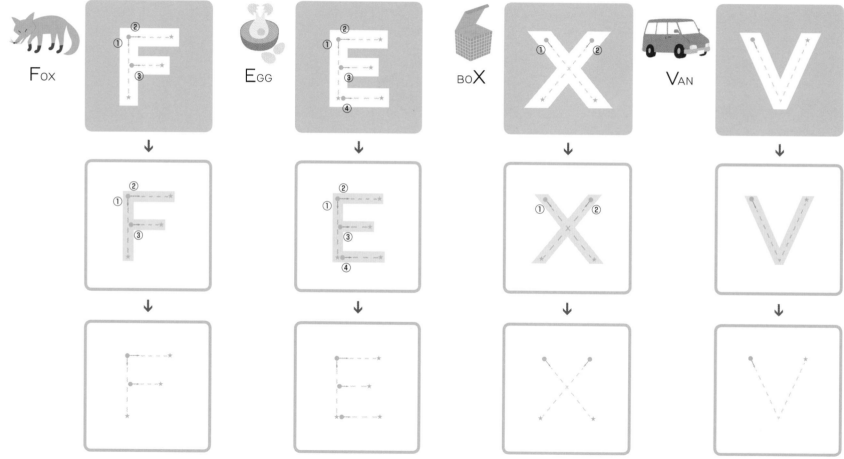

Fox    Egg    boX    Van

# Review: Writing Y, N, Z, and A

Name

Date

■ Read the words aloud and trace the letters. Follow the order of the numbers.

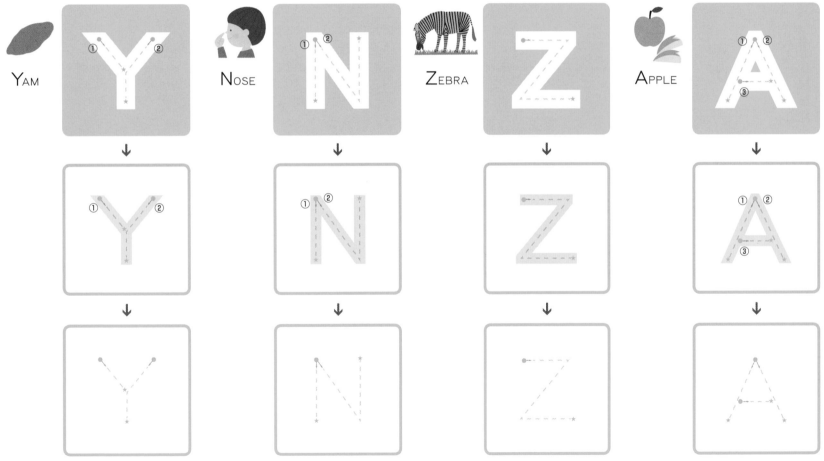

Yam  Nose  Zebra  Apple

# Review: Writing K, M, and W

■ Read the words aloud and trace the letters. Follow the order of the numbers.

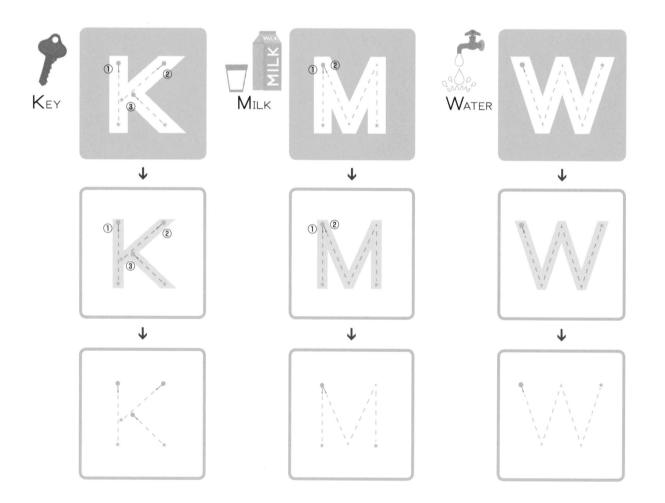

# Curved Lines

Name

Date

■ Draw a line from one picture to the matching picture.

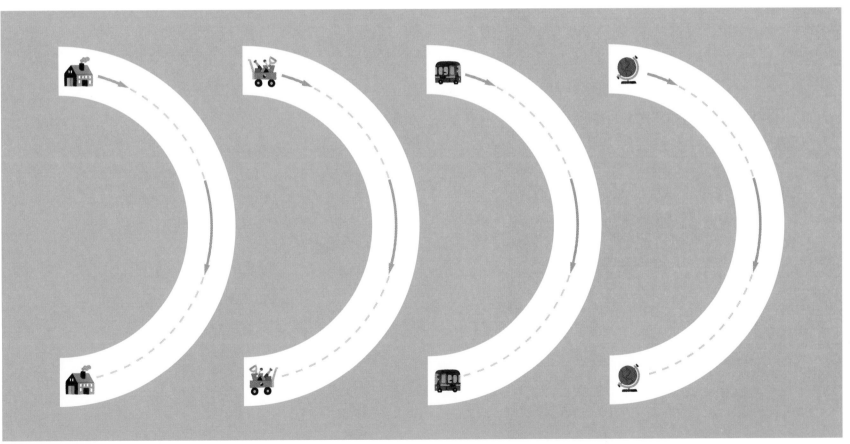

■ Draw a line from one picture to the matching picture.

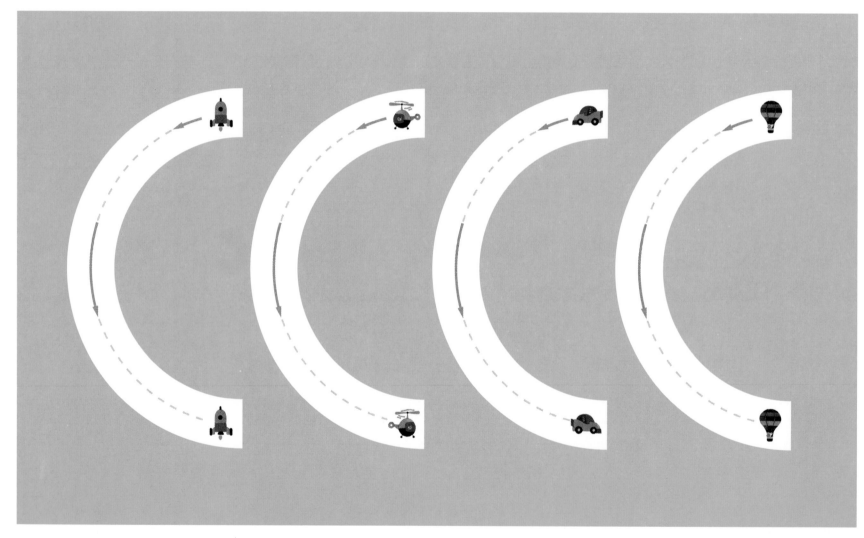

## Writing D

■ Read the word aloud and trace the letters. Follow the order of the numbers.

D  DOG

| A | B | C | D | E | F | G | H | I | J | K | L | M | N | O | P | Q | R | S | T | U | V | W | X | Y | Z |

# Writing P

■ Read the word aloud and trace the letters. Follow the order of the numbers.

P PAN

A B C D E F G H I J K L M N O P Q R S T U V W X Y Z

## Writing B

■ Read the word aloud and trace the letters. Follow the order of the numbers.

B  BAG

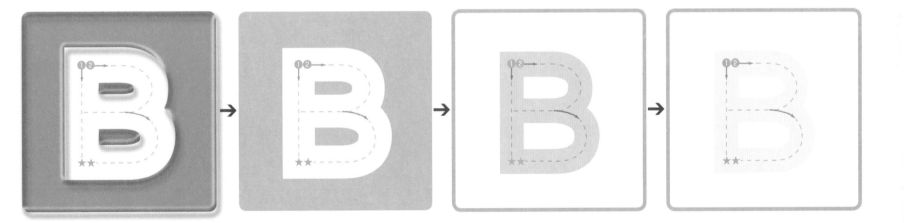

A B C D E F G H I J K L M N O P Q R S T U V W X Y Z

# Writing D, P, and B

■ Read the words aloud and trace the letters. Follow the order of the numbers.

Dog

Pan

Bag

Name

Date

■ Read the word aloud and trace the letters. Follow the order of the numbers.

R  RING

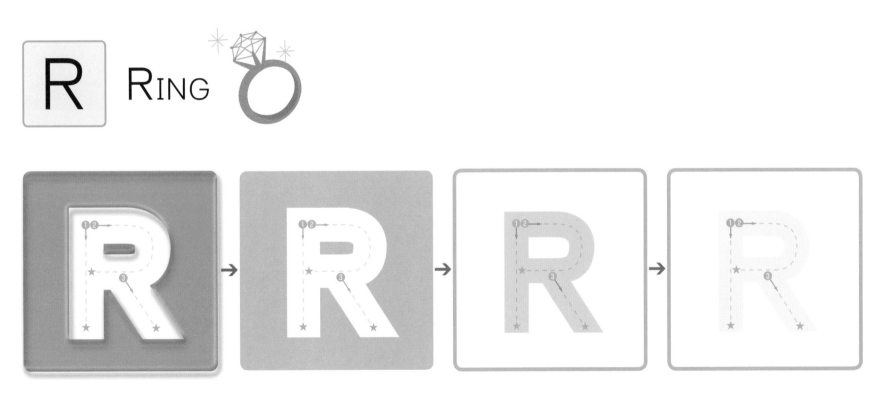

A B C D E F G H I J K L M N O P Q R S T U V W X Y Z

# Writing J

- Read the word aloud and trace the letters.

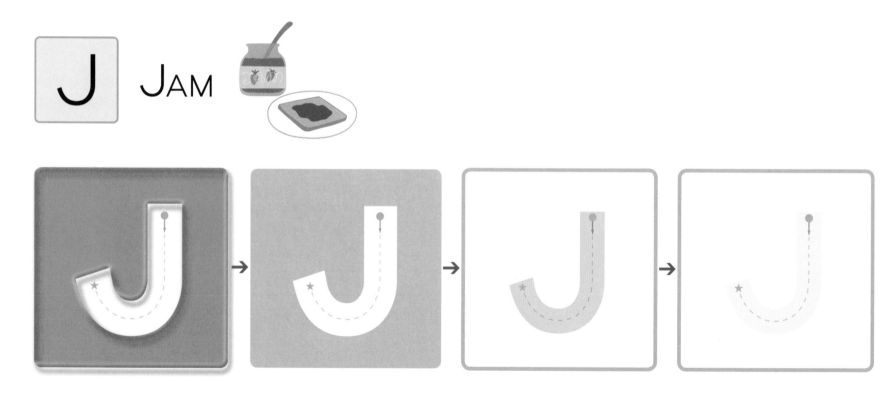

J  JAM

| A | B | C | D | E | F | G | H | I | J | K | L | M | N | O | P | Q | R | S | T | U | V | W | X | Y | Z |

| Name | |
|------|--|
| Date | |

■ Read the word aloud and trace the letters.

U UMBRELLA

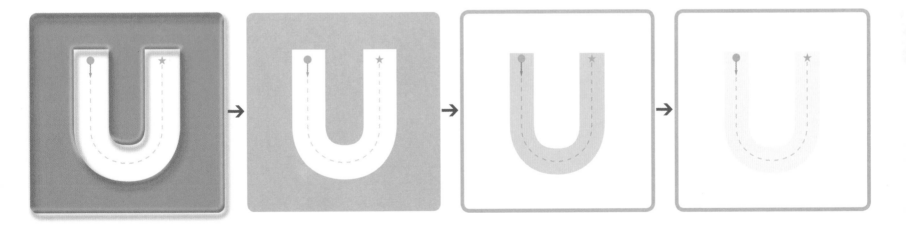

A B C D E F G H I J K L M N O P Q R S T U V W X Y Z

# Writing R, J, and U

■ Read the words aloud and trace the letters. Follow the order of the numbers.

RING

JAM

UMBRELLA

# 22 Curved Lines

Draw a line from one picture to the matching picture.

■ Draw a line from one picture to the matching picture.

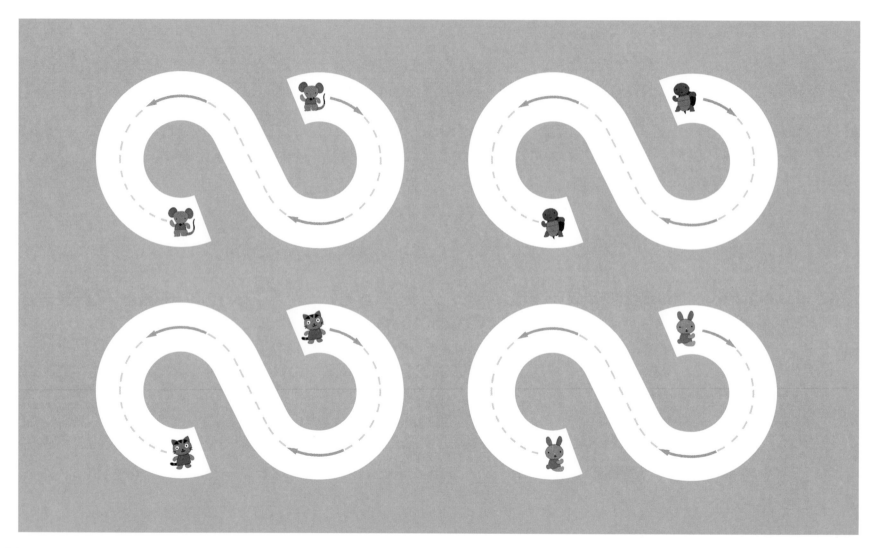

# Writing C

Name

Date

■ Read the word aloud and trace the letters.

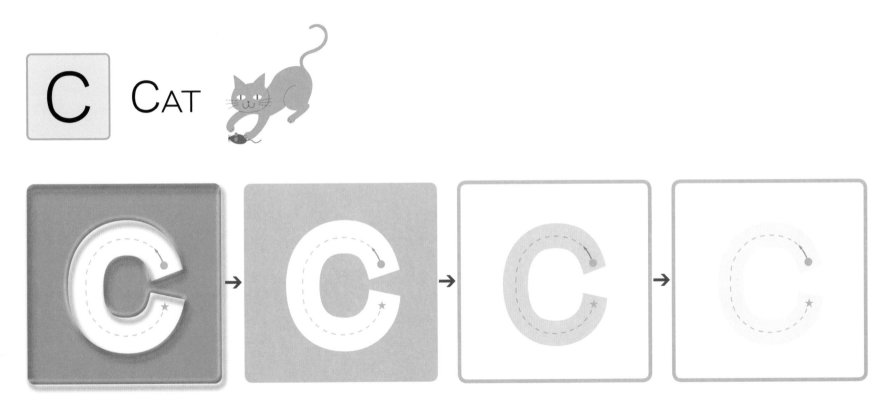

C  CAT

A B C D E F G H I J K L M N O P Q R S T U V W X Y Z

# Writing G

■ Read the word aloud and trace the letters. Follow the order of the numbers.

 G GIFT

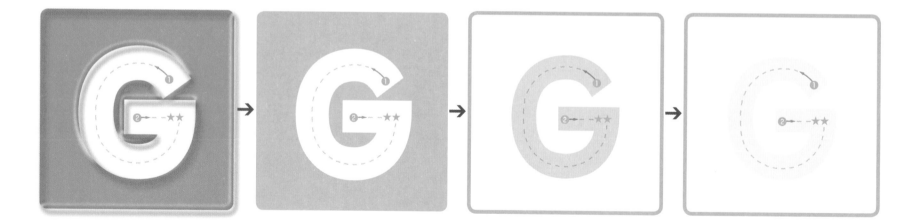

| A | B | C | D | E | F | G | H | I | J | K | L | M | N | O | P | Q | R | S | T | U | V | W | X | Y | Z |

## Writing S

Name

Date

■ Read the word aloud and trace the letters.

S SUN

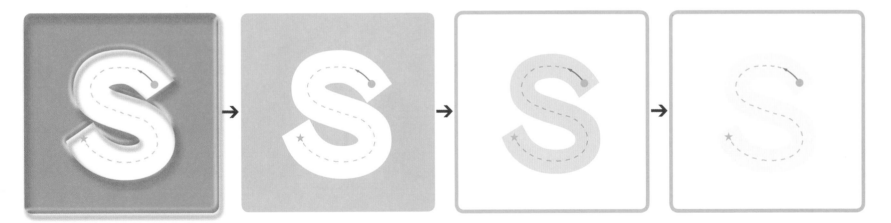

A B C D E F G H I J K L M N O P Q R S T U V W X Y Z

# Writing C, G, and S

■ Read the words aloud and trace the letters. Follow the order of the numbers.

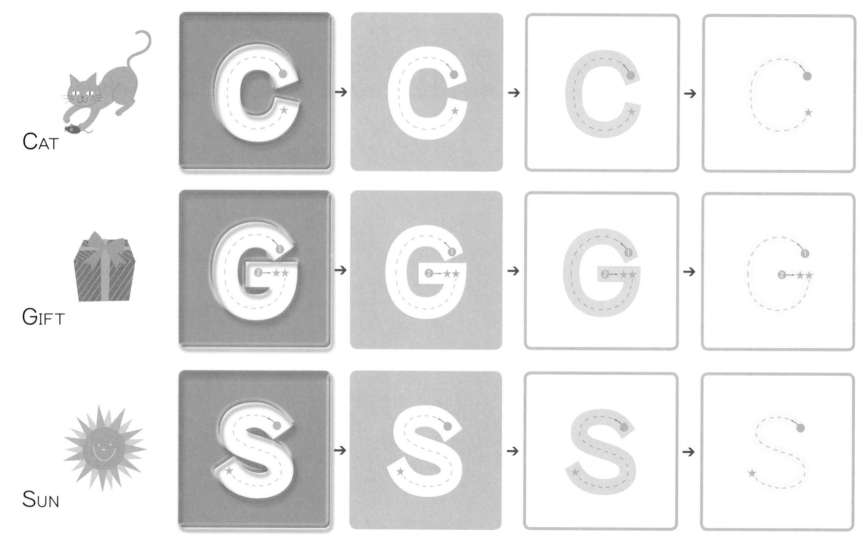

CAT

GIFT

SUN

Name

Date

■ Draw a line from one picture to the matching picture.

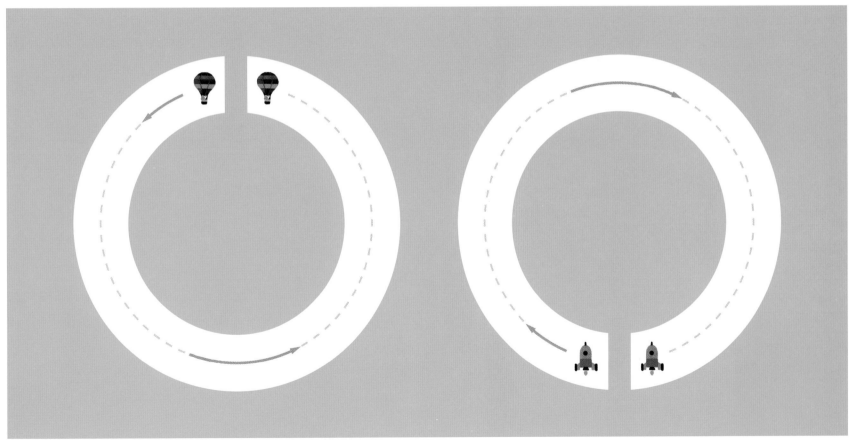

■ Draw a line from one picture to the matching picture.

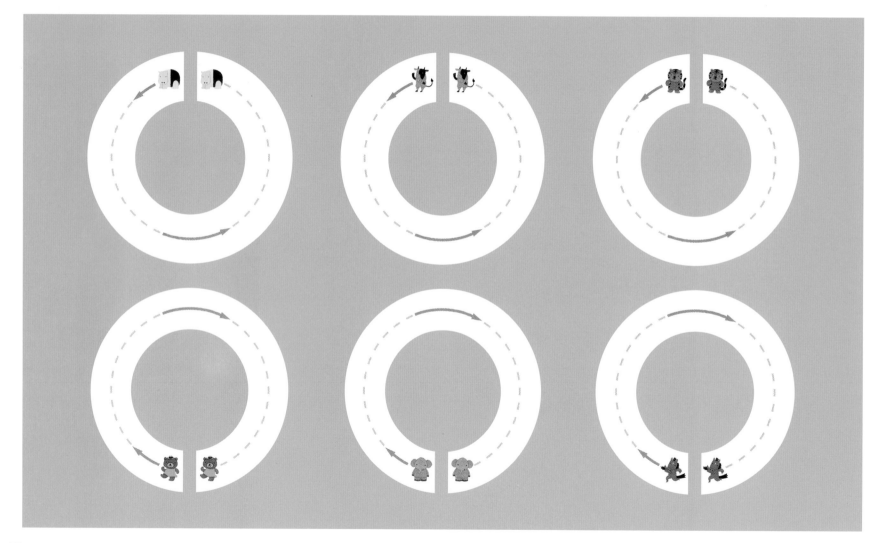

## Writing O

**26 Writing O**

Name

Date

■ Read the word aloud and trace the letters.

O ORANGE

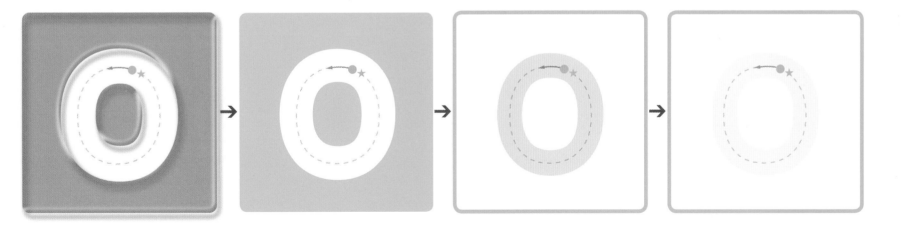

A B C D E F G H I J K L M N O P Q R S T U V W X Y Z

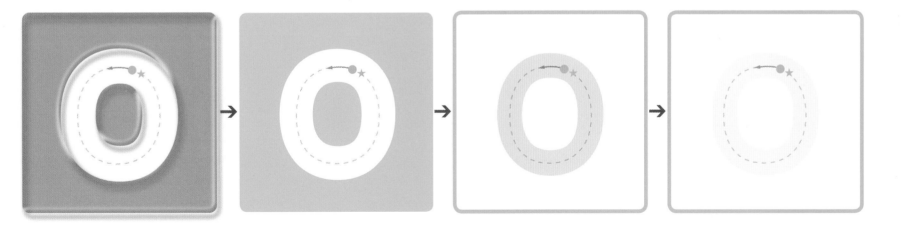

51

# Writing Q

■ Read the word aloud and trace the letters. Follow the order of the numbers.

Q  QUEEN

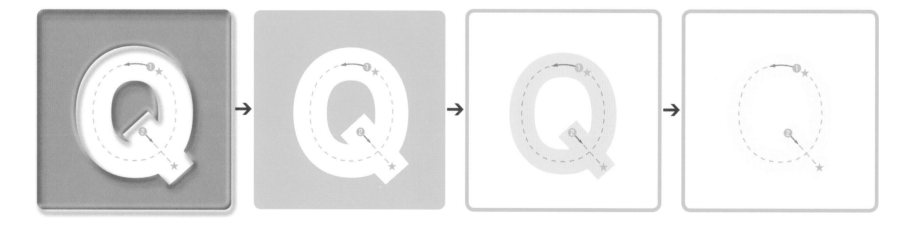

| A | B | C | D | E | F | G | H | I | J | K | L | M | N | O | P | Q | R | S | T | U | V | W | X | Y | Z |

# Writing O and Q

■ Read the words aloud and trace the letters. Follow the order of the numbers.

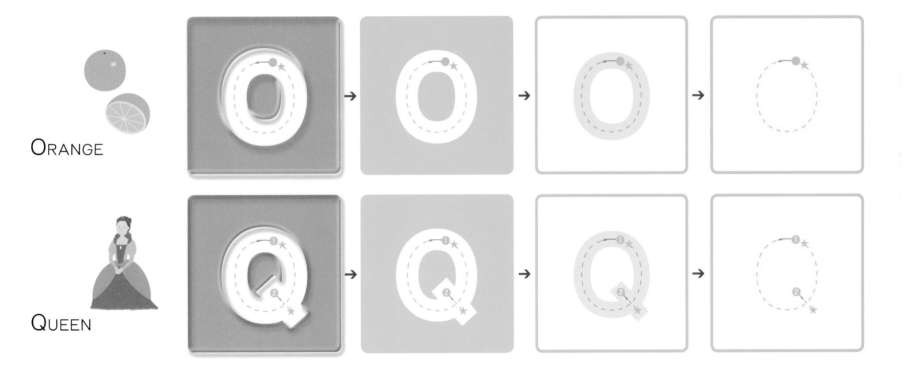

ORANGE

QUEEN

# Review: Writing D, P, B, and R

■ Read the words aloud and trace the letters. Follow the order of the numbers.

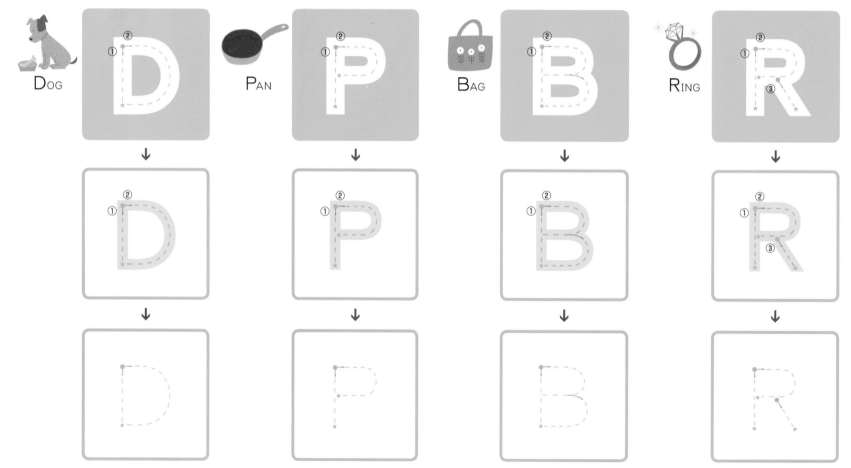

Dog    Pan    Bag    Ring

54

# Review: Writing J, U, C, and G

Name

Date

■ Read the words aloud and trace the letters. Follow the order of the numbers.

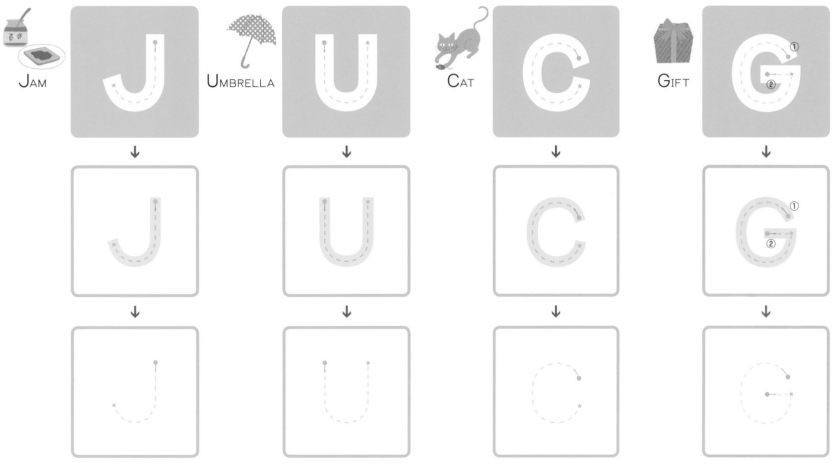

JAM  UMBRELLA  CAT  GIFT

# Review: Writing S, O, and Q

■ Read the words aloud and trace the letters. Follow the order of the numbers.

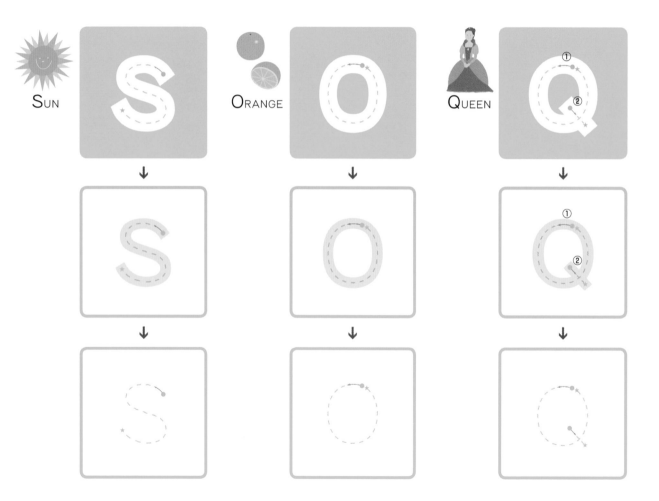

SUN    ORANGE    QUEEN

## 29 Review: Writing A to G

■ Say the sound of the letters A to G as you trace them.

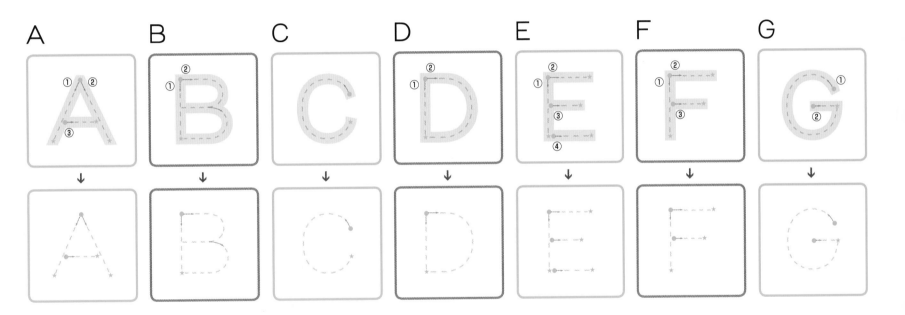

A B C D E F G H I J K L M N O P Q R S T U V W X Y Z

# Review: Writing H to N

■ Say the sound of the letters H to N as you trace them.

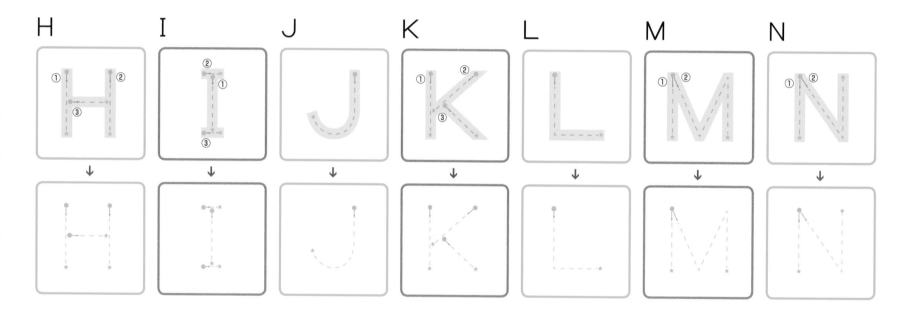

| A | B | C | D | E | F | G | H | I | J | K | L | M | N | O | P | Q | R | S | T | U | V | W | X | Y | Z |

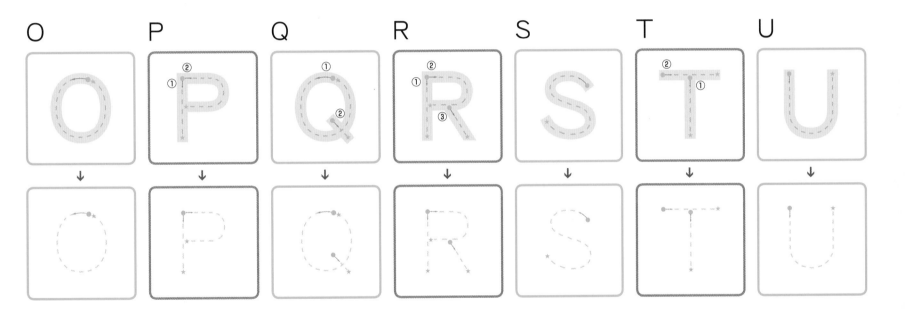

## Review: Writing O to U

**30**

Name

Date

■ Say the sound of the letters O to U as you trace them.

O    P    Q    R    S    T    U

| A | B | C | D | E | F | G | H | I | J | K | L | M | N | O | P | Q | R | S | T | U | V | W | X | Y | Z |

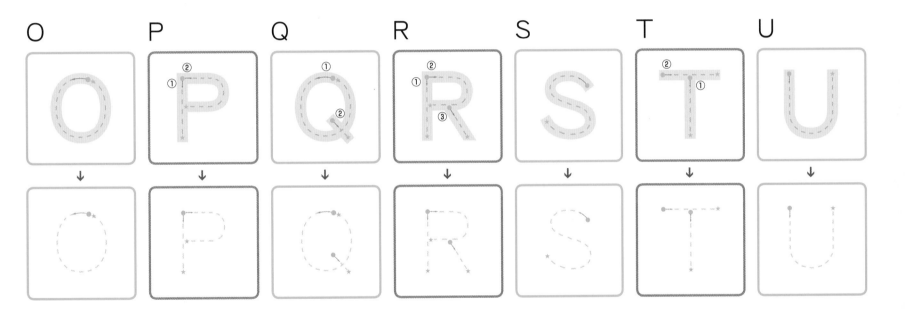

# Review: Writing V to Z

■ Say the sound of the letters V to Z as you trace them.

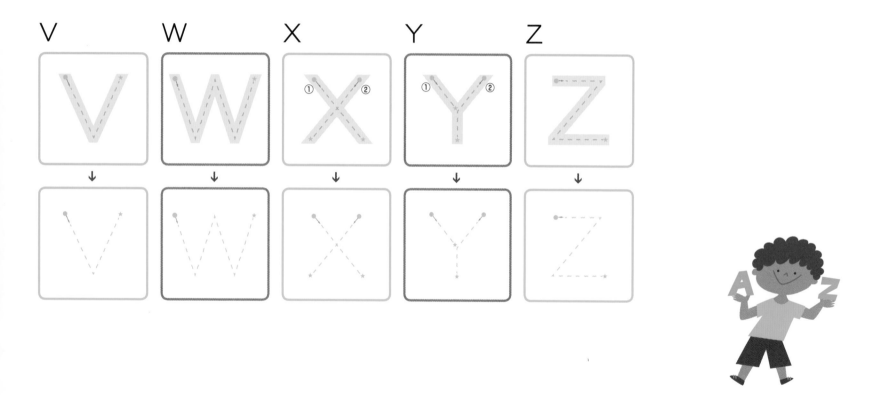

| A | B | C | D | E | F | G | H | I | J | K | L | M | N | O | P | Q | R | S | T | U | V | W | X | Y | Z |

# Review: Writing A to N

■ Say the sound of the letters A to N as you trace them.

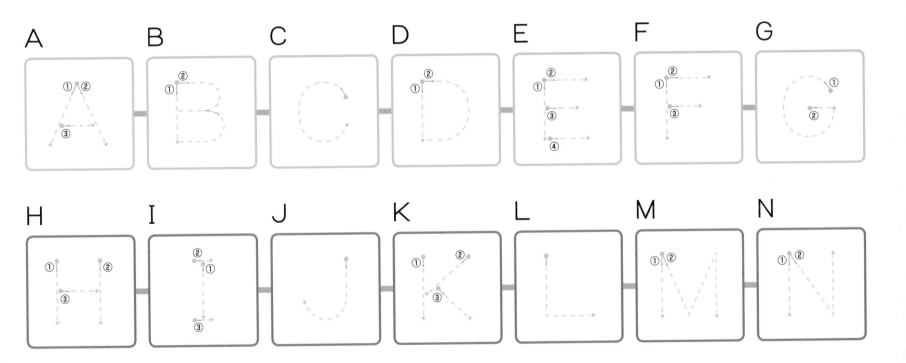

# Review: Writing O to Z

■ Say the sound of the letters O to Z as you trace them.

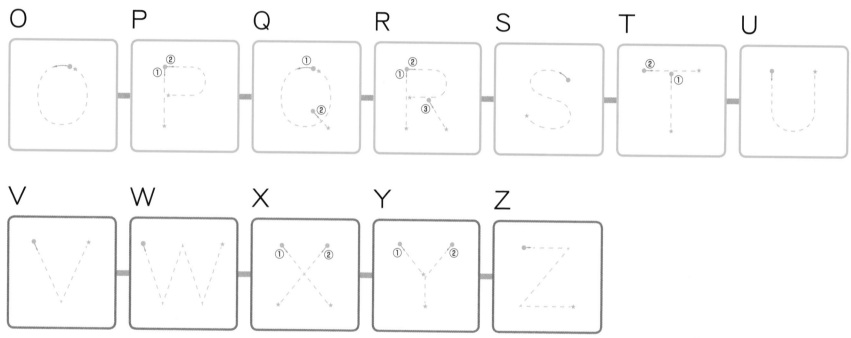

# Review: Writing A to Z

Name

Date

■ Trace the letters A to Z.

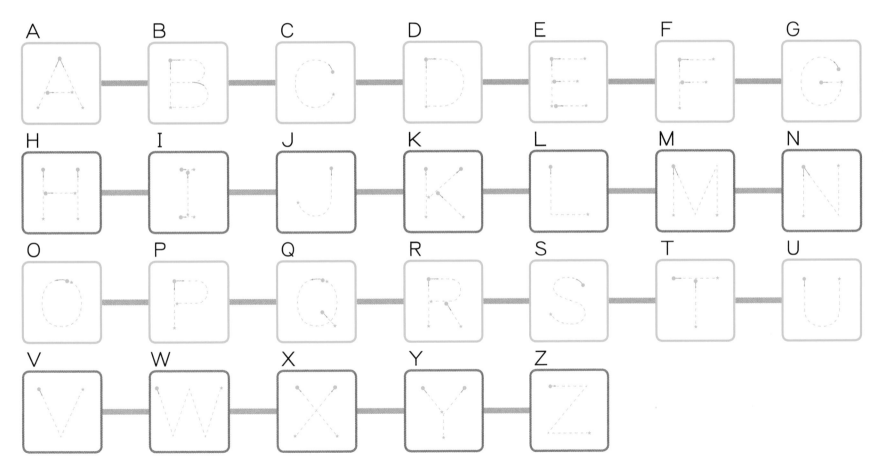

# Review: Writing A to Z

**To parents**
Please praise your child for the effort it took to complete this workbook. If he or she has mastered reading and recognizing the shapes of uppercase letters, your child should practice writing the letters with words.

■ Write the letters A to Z.

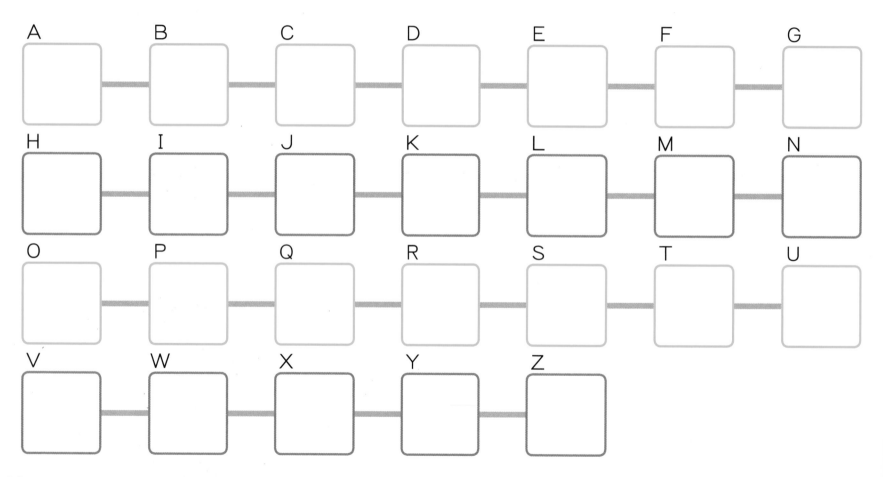

A   B   C   D   E   F   G

H   I   J   K   L   M   N

O   P   Q   R   S   T   U

V   W   X   Y   Z